W0259724

Elli Woollard

Life

Illustrated by

Dorien Brouwers

PUFFIN

In the time before time,
when the world had its birth,

There was *nothing*
that lived on the whole of the **Earth.**

This new-formed world, an unwelcoming place,
Was bombarded by rocks from far across space;
By fearsome comets with tearing tails
And meteorites in blazing trails,

Which whirled through the vastness of dark to smash
On the face of the Earth with a thundering

CRASH.

For millions of years, the Earth was battered,
Until, with one blow, the planet was shattered.
Rocks were blasted and broke away
To become the moon, small and grey.

Then the Earth was on fire, a **big** burning ball,

Too hot and too poisonous for life at all.

But soon, with the orbiting moon in tow,
The spinning of Earth began to slow,

And the planet now tilted sideways to bring
The winter, summer, autumn, spring.

Then water vapour condensed and cooled
To form droplets and streams, which grew and pooled
Into seas that swelled with a rush and a roar
To CRASH on the edge of the lonely shore
Of the very first lands which began to arise,
Vast and bare under hostile skies.

Raging volcanoes now started to mass,
Spewing out spluttering fire and gas
In torrents of smoke and noxious fumes
And bursts of lava in blasting booms,
As all around the wild waves surged.
Until out of these seas the first life emerged.

Tiny bacteria, spreading unseen,
Till the waters were speckled with freckles of green.
These dots breathed oxygen into the seas,
Then into the air, so the billowing breeze
And the whole of the Earth's wide atmosphere
Was filled with the stuff for new life to appear.

Strange creatures arose in the seas' soft swells;
Tree-like sponges, tubes with shells,
Spiny blobs, worms with fins,
Flat round discs with armoured skins,
Gigantic beasts with spikes to crush
And turn their prey to pulp and mush,
Till the oceans writhed and wiggled and whirled
With wonderful life, as the waters swirled.

For millions of years as the planet revolved
These creatures changed, adapted, evolved:
Slithering slim-finned sharp-toothed sharks
That lurked in the oceans' depths and darks,
And new ones appeared: the bony fishes
That slid through the seas with gentle swishes.

Then some things emerged with four legs, to stand
On the golden floor of the sea-bed sand,
Until out of the oceans, wide and deep,
These creatures began to crawl and creep
On sliding, gliding, new-found feet,
And breathed in the air, fresh and sweet.

On land they found forests of dense green trees,
Towering tall in the steamy breeze,
And swamps which the creatures squelched across,
Lush with feathery fern and moss.
But still, these creatures that slid on four legs
Returned to the water to lay their eggs.

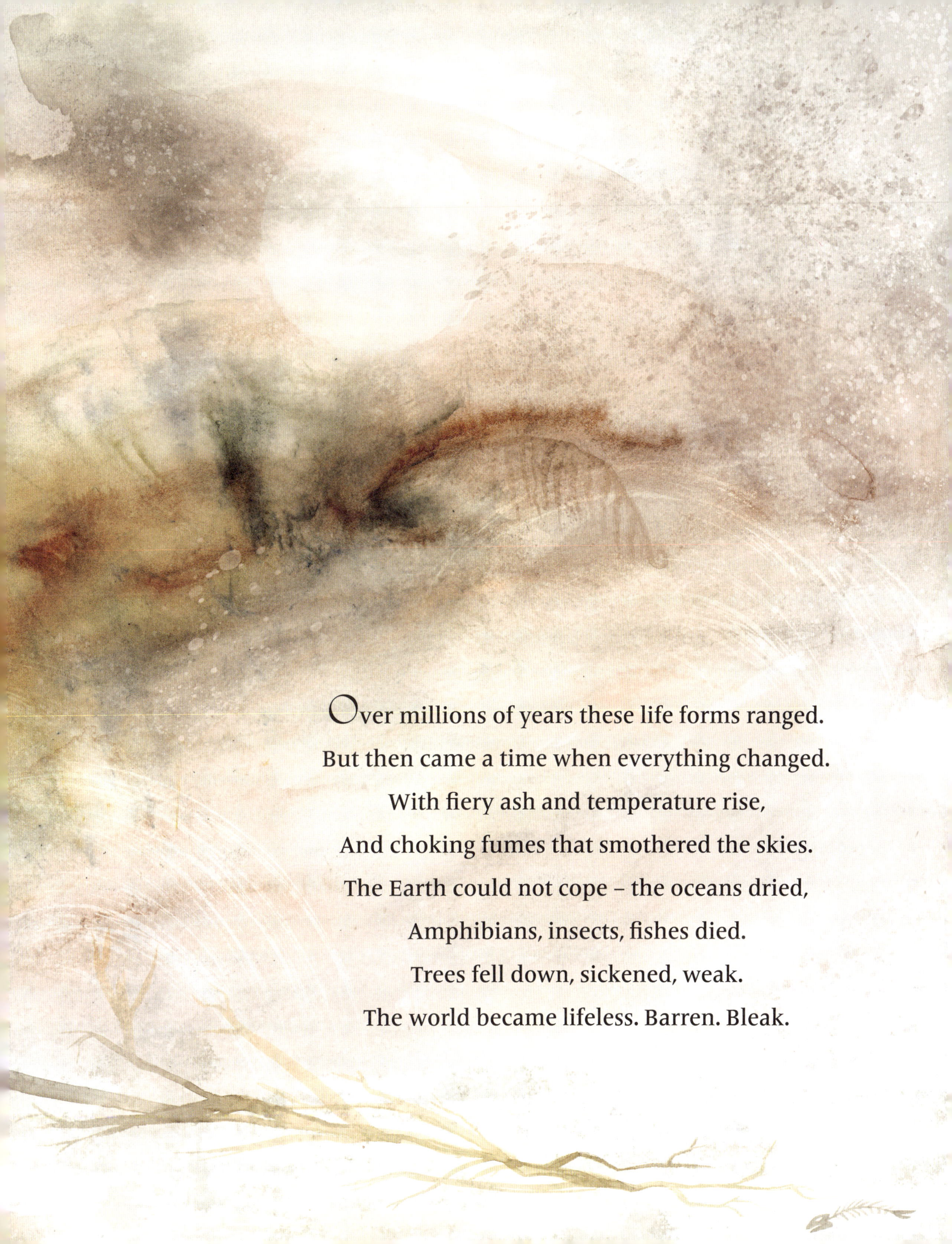

Over millions of years these life forms ranged.
But then came a time when everything changed.
With fiery ash and temperature rise,
And choking fumes that smothered the skies.
The Earth could not cope – the oceans dried,
Amphibians, insects, fishes died.
Trees fell down, sickened, weak.
The world became lifeless. Barren. Bleak.

LIFELESS?

No, not all was gone.

A few of the creatures struggled on,
Adapting to live in the desert sands
That stretched over desolate empty lands.
Thick-skinned things with hardened scales
And thrashing, lashing, slashing tails.
Stocky creatures with powerful claws
And gripping, ripping, beak-like jaws.
Beasts with a long and tube-shaped snout,
And ones that lived quite well without.
Creatures that took to the air and flew
In scorching skies of vibrant blue –

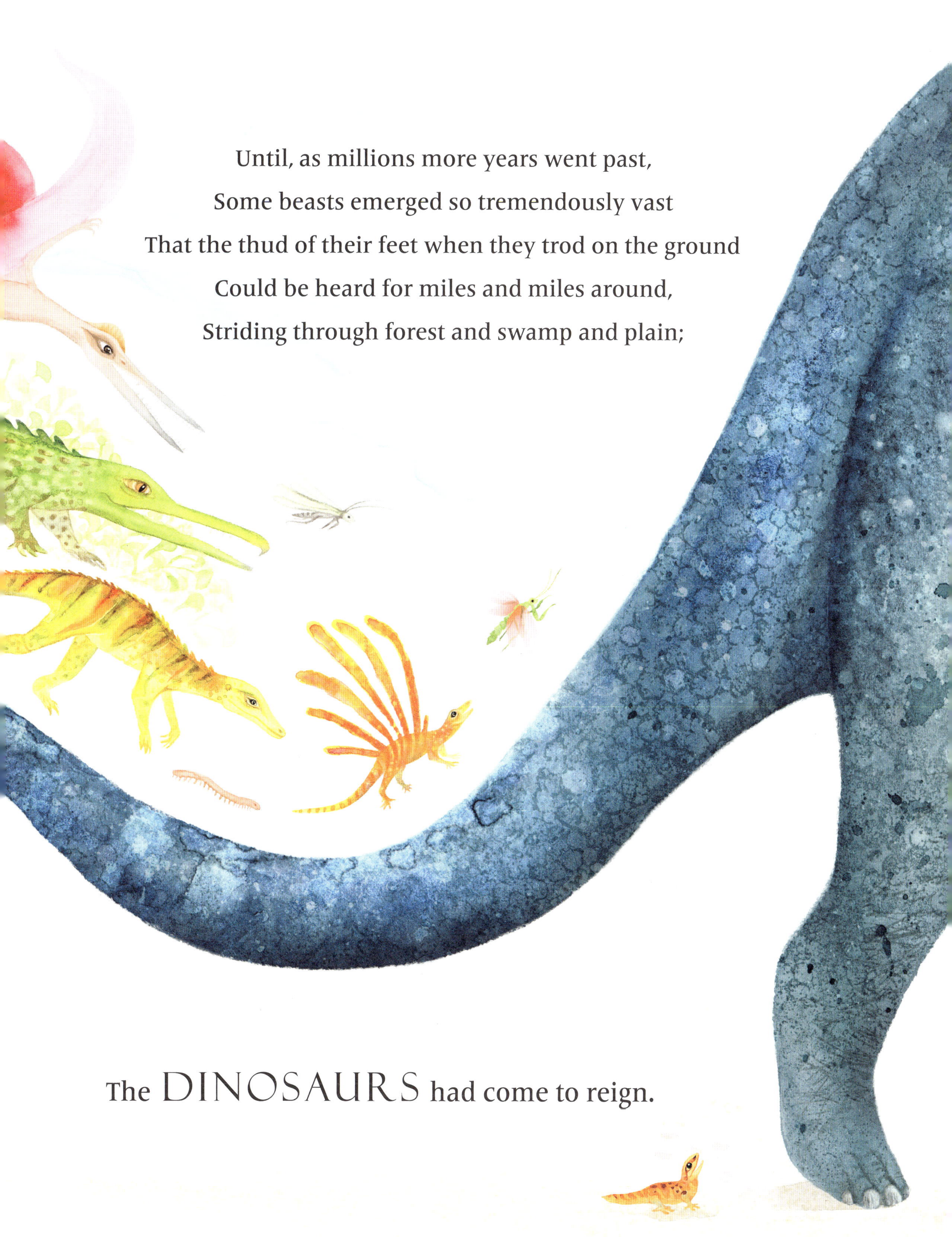

Until, as millions more years went past,
Some beasts emerged so tremendously vast
That the thud of their feet when they trod on the ground
Could be heard for miles and miles around,
Striding through forest and swamp and plain;

The DINOSAURS had come to reign.

Dinosaurs. Every imaginable sort:
Tiny ones, chunky ones, tall ones, short.
Gnawing ones, clawing ones, tearing up meat.
Gentle ones, chewing fresh leaves to eat.

Some with spikes standing tall on their backs,
Others with horns, perhaps for attacks,
Some who stomped, stumpy and stout,
Others who darted and dashed about,

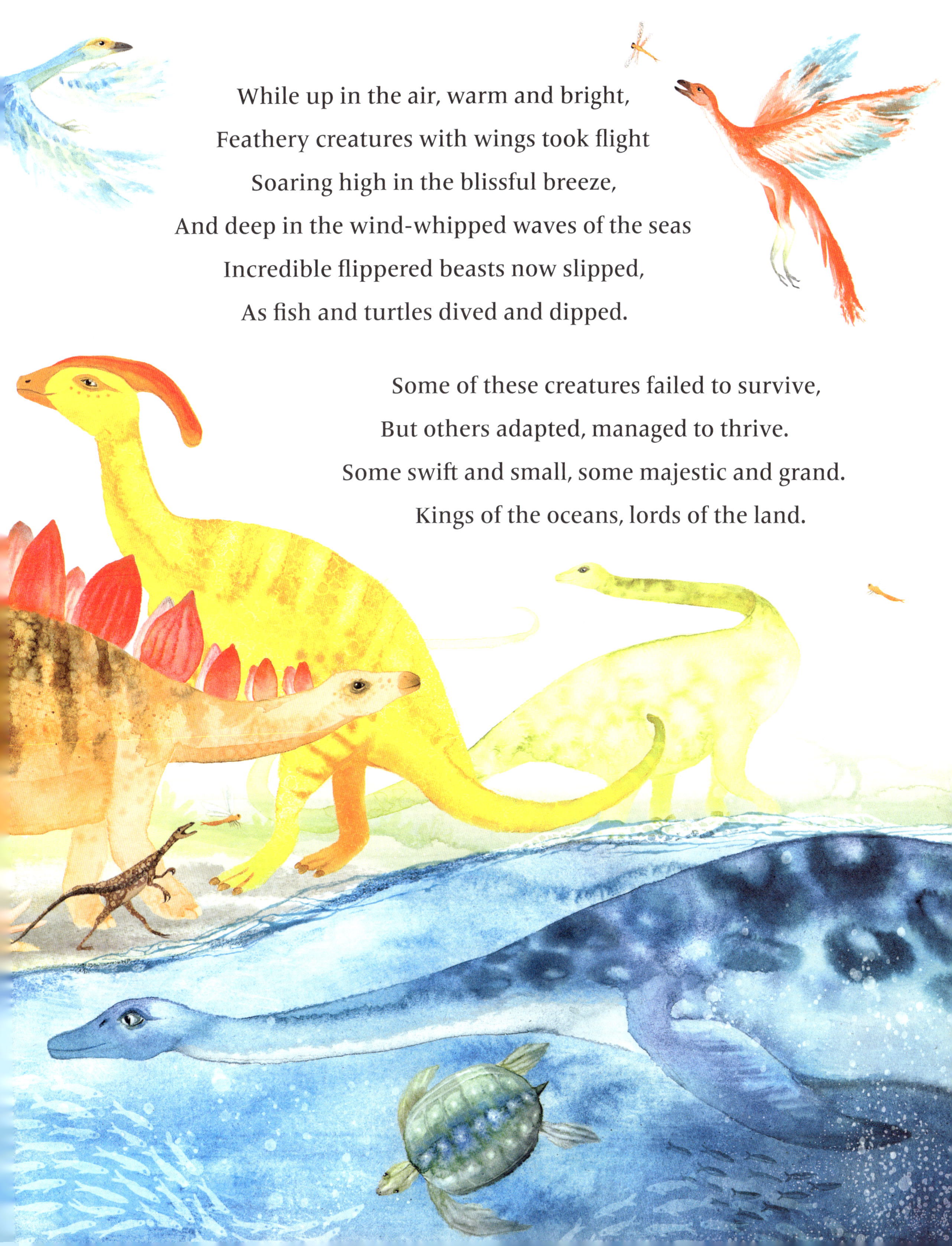

While up in the air, warm and bright,
Feathery creatures with wings took flight
Soaring high in the blissful breeze,
And deep in the wind-whipped waves of the seas
Incredible flippered beasts now slipped,
As fish and turtles dived and dipped.

Some of these creatures failed to survive,
But others adapted, managed to thrive.
Some swift and small, some majestic and grand.
Kings of the oceans, lords of the land.

As many more millions of years went by
Long-plumed birds now took to the sky,
Filling the air with their wings' loud whirr.
Mammals appeared, downy with fur,

On plants, the very first flowers unfurled,
Their blooms bursting forth in the sunlit world,
And the blossoming breath of the sweet-scented breeze
Was alive with the hum and the thrum of bees.

While trees bore fruit, juicy and round,
Which ripened and fell, soft on the ground.

Yet in forest and swamp, in plain and on hill,
The dinosaurs ruled their kingdoms still,
With their terrible talons to rip and tear
Or necks that reared up high in the air,
Ones who had tails for bludgeoning blows
Or ones with horns on the end of their nose.
Magnificent creatures, beasts in their prime.

Yet perhaps they'd have seen, near the end of that time,
If they glanced in the star-sprinkled skies at night
Hurtling towards them, blazing bright . . .

An asteroid so wide, so vast,
That when it crashed down, the force of its blast
Turned all the Earth black, blocking the sun.

The dinosaurs died, one by one.

No more would they roam from shore to shore.
No more their stomps. No more their roar.
Buried with swamp and soil and stone,
These beasts became nothing but dust and bone.

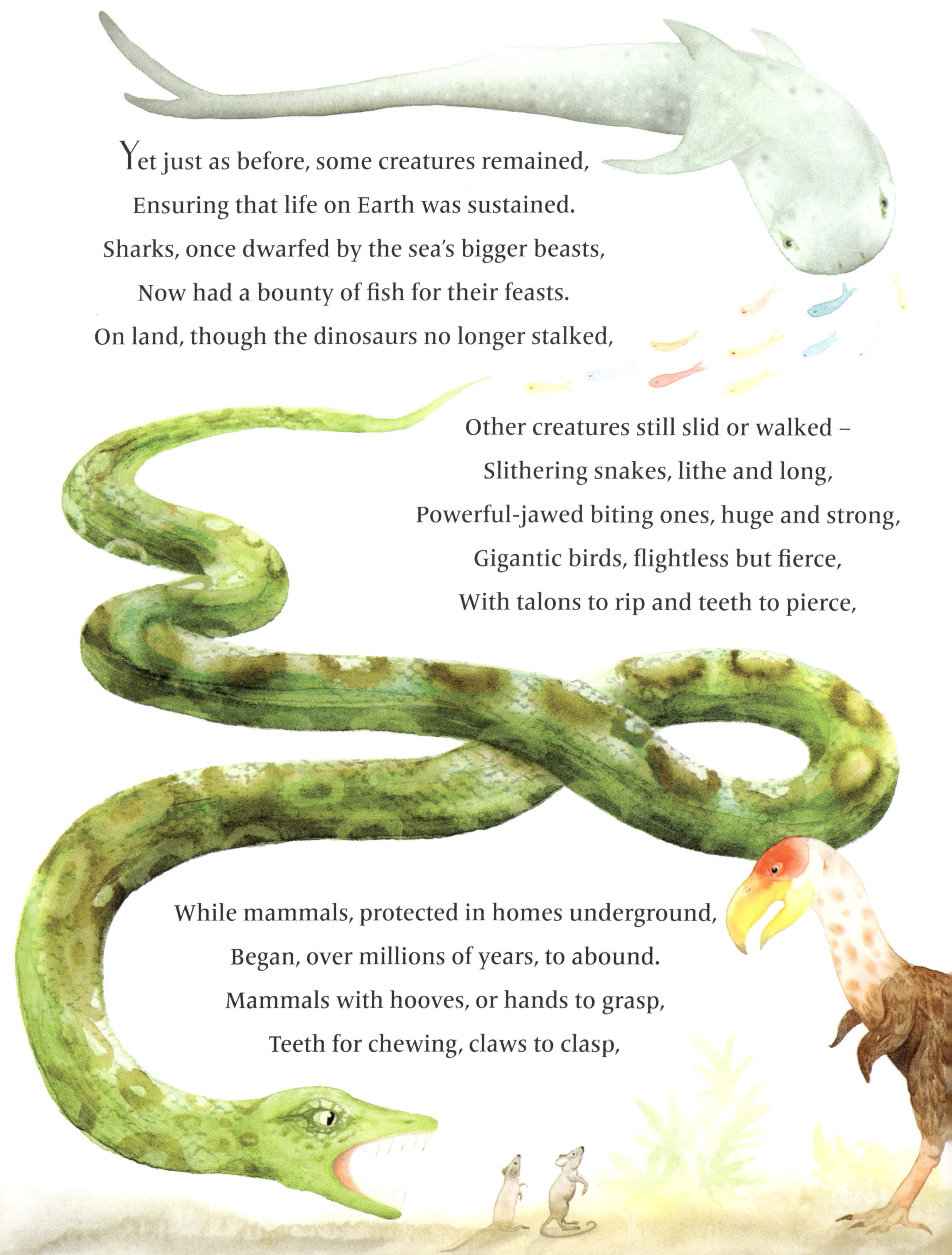

Yet just as before, some creatures remained,
Ensuring that life on Earth was sustained.
Sharks, once dwarfed by the sea's bigger beasts,
Now had a bounty of fish for their feasts.
On land, though the dinosaurs no longer stalked,

Other creatures still slid or walked –
Slithering snakes, lithe and long,
Powerful-jawed biting ones, huge and strong,
Gigantic birds, flightless but fierce,
With talons to rip and teeth to pierce,

While mammals, protected in homes underground,
Began, over millions of years, to abound.
Mammals with hooves, or hands to grasp,
Teeth for chewing, claws to clasp,

Ranging through grasslands, fresh and new,
Pearled with droplets of morning dew.
Some remained small, to be preyed on and eaten,

While others grew huge, unchallenged, unbeaten –
Tusked and trunked ones,
Ones built for racing,
Ones made for swimming,
And ones built for chasing,
Colossal great creatures, slow and slumbering,
Huge armoured animals, heavy and lumbering.

Some died out, but others lived longer –
Adapting, evolving, surviving, stronger.
Bears, beavers, dogs, deer,
Apes and whales now began to appear,
Gradually changing, bit by bit,

As once-joined lands grew rifts and split,
Or pushed together, thrusting high
In mountains that reached to the roof of the sky.

Some apes who traipsed across the land
Eventually came to rise and stand
Not on four feet, but rather on two,
And found there were so many things they could do:
Grasp with their hands to make tools of stone,
Of wood or antler, shell or bone,
Make shelters to keep themselves dry and warm
In biting winds and lashing storm.
And now, with tools they could hunt their prey,
Striking with spears from far away.

In time, these creatures started to roam
Far from the lands of their African home,
Using animal skins as simple clothes
As the world around them cooled and froze.
And the creatures that thrived and didn't get sick

Were the ones who grew fur that was warm and thick;
Rhinos and mammoths with wool-covered skins,
Fleet-footed cats with sabre-toothed grins,
Deer with antlers as tall as the trees,
Which shivered in icy blasts of breeze.

In turn, these animals too disappeared,
Killed by warming, or hunted and speared
Until apes emerged who were cleverer still,
Filled with perception, reason and skill;

Humans, who used their complex brains
To trek the expanse of African plains.

Through desert, river, mountain, wood,
Spreading and settling wherever they could.
As so they came to understand

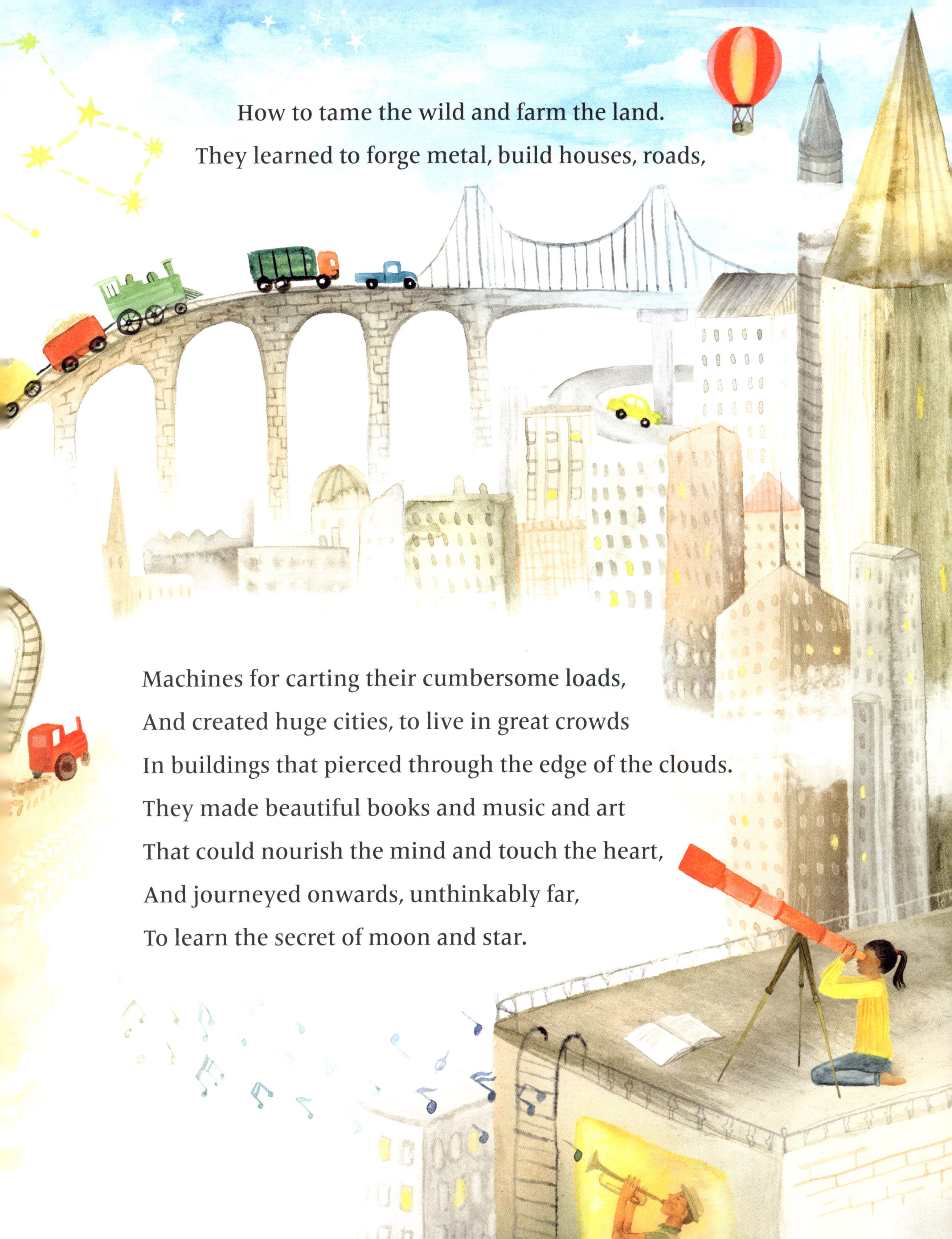

How to tame the wild and farm the land.
They learned to forge metal, build houses, roads,

Machines for carting their cumbersome loads,
And created huge cities, to live in great crowds
In buildings that pierced through the edge of the clouds.
They made beautiful books and music and art
That could nourish the mind and touch the heart,
And journeyed onwards, unthinkably far,
To learn the secret of moon and star.

But we humans began to think we could live
By taking more than the Earth could give.
We wrecked the soil, we chopped down trees,
Dumped our waste on land and in seas.

We pumped pollution into the skies
Causing air to heat and oceans to rise,
So that plants and animals, priceless, distinct,
Disappeared forever, vanished, extinct.

The world became sick, a suffering place,
And all because of the human race –
The very first creatures on Earth to enjoy
This terrible power to build and destroy,
The power to despoil and the power to end.

BUT ALSO THE
POWER
TO BEGIN TO MEND

The power to come together as one
And learn how to heal the damage we've done.
The power to love and remember the worth . . .

Of this precious place –
our home,
PLANET EARTH.

LIFE – A VERY BRIEF HISTORY

Life on Earth has **evolved** (very gradually changed and adapted) over billions of years. Many forms of life that once lived have become **extinct** (they no longer have any living members). Over history there have been five **mass extinctions** (events caused by natural disasters such as asteroids or extreme temperature changes when a large number of living things become extinct within a short space of time). Modern humans have only lived on Earth for 300,000 years, but human-made climate change is now causing the **sixth mass extinction.**

About 4.6 billion years ago
Planet Earth is formed from gas and dust in space.

About 4.51 billion years ago
Earth's moon forms after a huge collision with another planet causes part of the Earth to break away.

By 3.8 billion years ago
The first water appears on Earth. Water may have existed as early as 4.4 billion years ago.

About 3.7 billion years ago
The first life has emerged, in the form of microbes (extremely tiny living things).

About 2.5 billion years ago
Cyanobacteria (blue-green algae) evolves, converting sunlight into oxygen in a process known as photosynthesis. Cyanobacteria releases a large amount of oxygen into the atmosphere, allowing complex life to develop.

About 760 million years ago
The first animals evolve in the sea.

About 530 million years ago
The first fish evolve. These were the first vertebrates (animals with backbones).

About 500 million years ago
The first plants evolve on land. The first insects evolve at around the same time.

Scientists are constantly learning more about Earth, and coming up with new discoveries about its history. The figures in this book are based on scientific **hypotheses** (guesses made using the evidence we have available), but can never be precise, and not all scientists will agree with all of them. Our understanding of exactly when and how key events happened will almost certainly change in the future as our knowledge grows. Perhaps one day you will make important discoveries too.

About 365 million years ago
The first land vertebrates appear.

About 252 million years ago
Once of the worst mass extinctions (the third in Earth's history) kill up to 96% of all species (distinct groups of living things).

About 245 million years ago
The first dinosaurs evolve.

About 225 million years ago
The first mammals evolve.

About 160 million years ago
The first birds evolve.

About 130 million years ago
The first flowering plants appear.

About 66 million years ago
Most dinosaurs are made extinct as a result of a meteorite crashing into Earth. A few species of dinosaurs survive, and evolve into our modern birds.

About 10 million years ago
The first hominids (a group of species that eventually evolve into apes and humans) evolve.

About 2 million years ago
Homo erectus (a hominid ancestor of modern humans) start to migrate out of Africa.

About 300,000 years ago
The first modern humans (Homo sapiens) appear.

To all the children of today and tomorrow,
inheritors of our beautiful and fragile planet – E. W.

To Mae, who asked if a dinosaur has ever given birth to a human
And to William, my little eco-warrior – D. B.

With thanks to Dr Nick Crumpton

PUFFIN BOOKS

UK | USA | Canada | Ireland | Australia | India | New Zealand | South Africa

Puffin Books is part of the Penguin Random House group of companies
whose addresses can be found at global.penguinrandomhouse.com.

www.penguin.co.uk www.puffin.co.uk www.ladybird.co.uk

First published 2023

001

Printed and bound in China

The authorized representative in the EEA is Penguin Random House Ireland, Morrison Chambers, 32 Nassau Street, Dublin D02 YH68

A CIP catalogue record for this book is available from the British Library

ISBN: 978-0-241-45286-8

All correspondence to:
Puffin Books, Penguin Random House Children's, One Embassy Gardens, 8 Viaduct Gardens, London SW11 7BW